Silent Films to 3D Movies
Then to Now Tech

By Jennifer Colby

21st Century
Junior Library

Published in the United States of America by
Cherry Lake Publishing
Ann Arbor, Michigan
www.cherrylakepublishing.com

Content Adviser: Adam Fulton Johnson, PhD History of Science and Technology, University of Michigan
Reading Adviser: Marla Conn, MS, Ed., Literacy specialist, Read-Ability, Inc.

Library of Congress Cataloging-in-Publication Data
Names: Colby, Jennifer, 1971- author.
Title: Silent films to 3D movies / Jennifer Colby.
Description: Ann Arbor : Cherry Lake Publishing, [2019] | Series: Then to now tech |
    Includes bibliographical references and index.
Identifiers: LCCN 2019004228| ISBN 9781534147232 (hardcover) | ISBN
    9781534148666 (pdf) | ISBN 9781534150096 (pbk.) | ISBN 9781534151529
    (hosted ebook)
Subjects: LCSH: Cinematography—History—Juvenile literature.
Classification: LCC TR851 .C56 2019 | DDC 777—dc23
LC record available at https://lccn.loc.gov/2019004228

Cherry Lake Publishing would like to acknowledge the work of the Partnership for 21st Century Skills.
Please visit *www.p21.org* for more information.

Printed in the United States of America
Corporate Graphics

CONTENTS

Lobby cards are like miniature movie posters. They give viewers a sneak peek of a scene in the film.

On the Big Screen

You have seen a movie. But can you imagine watching a movie without hearing the actors speak? That is what early movies were: silent. Sound technology hadn't been invented. Moving images were recorded on **film** and **projected** onto a screen. A pianist or orchestra played music to accompany the movie. In 1895, the Lumière brothers of France showed silent films in Paris. They were among the first **filmmakers** in history.

Theaters were grand. New theaters opened just for films.

A Star Is Born

Silent films were usually a small part of a larger theatrical show. People loved going to see films, and the popularity of movies soon grew. Many stages where plays were normally presented became movie theaters. Stage actors became movie stars in **feature films**.

Mary Pickford was a silent film star and later a producer.
She was known as "America's Sweetheart" and won the second ever
Academy Award for Best Actress.

Without sound, actors had to be very **dramatic**. They emphasized their **facial expressions** and **body language**. This helped audiences understand how the actors were feeling. Words being said were shown on **title cards**.

Look!

Are you dramatic? Look in the mirror and make different facial expressions. Can you look sad? Can you look happy? What other feelings can you express?

Vitaphone was early movie sound equipment
made by Warner Bros.

Talkies and Technicolor

In the late 1920s, the first full-length movies were made with **synchronized** sound. Sound could be recorded directly onto the film or onto a sound **disc**. You could now hear what the actors were saying!

The success of "talkies" meant the end of silent films all around the world.

At first, sound recording was limited. Actors could not move around much. Cameras were noisy. And matching sound to what was happening on the screen was difficult. But soon these problems were solved, and all the major movie studios were making **talking pictures**.

The Wizard of Oz was an early movie made in full color.

Up until the 1930s, most full-length movies were filmed in black and white. Some **animated** movies were in color. But after the **invention** of new color film systems, almost all movies were filmed in color.

Make a Guess!

An early animation artist became one of the most popular filmmakers of all time. His studio released its first full-length color animated film in 1937. Who do you think it is? Ask an adult to help you find out.

A filming technique called *Cinerama* projected images from three cameras onto separate parts of the screen. Special theaters were made just for this technology.

Illusion of Reality

In the early 1950s, a wider movie screen helped to make the viewer feel part of the story. Later, a curved screen was introduced.

Think!

A filming technique still used today makes movies more realistic. You have to wear special glasses to see one of these movies. What type of movie do you think it is?

The special glasses you wear help the 3D movie come to life!

3D movies became popular in the 1950s. This type of movie requires filming with two cameras or one camera with two **lenses**. Each camera lens records a different view—just like the different views we see from our right eye and our left eye. The 3D image on the movie screen can only be seen while wearing special glasses.

Some movie theaters now show 4D movies. These movies have moving seats and wind and lighting effects to enhance the movie-watching experience.

You can interact with characters in your daily life.

What is the future for movies? **Augmented reality** (AR) could change the way you watch movies. Filmmakers are starting to combine recorded action with real-life situations. This technology could make movies more interactive and personalized.

Ask Questions!

Have you ever experienced augmented reality? If you have seen the first-down line on a televised football game or played *Pokémon GO*, then you have. Take a poll. Ask your friends and family if they have experienced augmented reality.

GLOSSARY

animated (AN-uh-may-tid) produced by the creation of a series of drawings that are shown quickly one after another

augmented reality (awg-MENT-id ree-AL-ih-tee) a technology that puts a computer-generated image on a user's view of the real world

body language (BAH-dee LANG-gwij) movements or positions of the body that express thoughts or feelings

disc (DISK) a flat, thin, round object

dramatic (druh-MAT-ik) showing a lot of emotion

facial expressions (FAY-shuhl ik-SPRESH-uhnz) muscle movements in the face that display emotions

feature films (FEE-chur FILMZ) full-length films that are the main event in a theater program

film (FILM) a special material that is used for recording images

filmmakers (FILM-may-kurz) people who make movies

invention (in-VEN-shun) something useful that is created or produced for the first time

lenses (LENZ-iz) clear curved pieces of glass used in cameras to capture images

projected (pruh-JEKT-id) displayed onto a surface from a distance

synchronized (SING-kruh-nized) happening at the same time

talking pictures (TAWK-ing PIK-churz) movies with synchronized sound

title cards (TYE-tuhl KARDZ) signs shown in a silent movie that display the action and words of a scene

FIND OUT MORE

BOOKS

McCully, Emily Arnold. *Strongheart: The World's First Movie Star Dog.* New York, NY: Henry Holt and Co., 2014.

Turner, Matt. *Genius Optical Inventions: From the X-ray to the Telescope.* Minneapolis, MN: Hungry Tomato, 2017.

WEBSITES

Science ABC—Science of 3D Movies: How Do Images on a Flat Screen Pop Out?
https://www.scienceabc.com/humans/science-of-3-d-movies-how-things-on-a-flat-screen-appear-to-emerge-depth.html
Learn the science behind 3D movies.

Smithsonian—O Say Can You See? Treasures from Hollywood's Silent Era
http://americanhistory.si.edu/blog/hollywoods-silent-era and
http://americanhistory.si.edu/blog/hollywoods-silent-era-2
Learn about the silent movie artifacts in the collection of the National Museum of American History.

INDEX

ABOUT THE AUTHOR

Jennifer Colby is a school librarian in Ann Arbor, Michigan. She loves reading, traveling, and going to museums to learn about new things.